FRANKENSTEIN

Adapted by
CHRISTINE DAVEY
Based on the novel by
MARY SHELLEY

CURRENCY PRESS
The performing arts publisher

CURRENT THEATRE SERIES

First published in 2023
by Currency Press Pty Ltd,
PO Box 2287, Strawberry Hills, NSW, 2012, Australia
enquiries@currency.com.au
www.currency.com.au

in association with La Mama

Copyright: *Frankenstein* © adapted by Christine Davey, based on the novel by Mary Shelley, 2023.

COPYING FOR EDUCATIONAL PURPOSES
The Australian *Copyright Act 1968* [Act] allows a maximum of one chapter or 10% of this book, whichever is the greater, to be copied by any educational institution for its educational purposes provided that that educational institution [or the body that administers it] has given a remuneration notice to Copyright Agency [CA] under the Act.
For details of the CA licence for educational institutions contact CA, 12/66 Goulburn Street, Sydney, NSW, 2000; tel: within Australia 1800 066 844 toll free; outside Australia 61 2 9394 7600; fax: 61 2 9394 7601; email: memberservices@copyright.com.au.

COPYING FOR OTHER PURPOSES
Except as permitted under the Act, for example a fair dealing for the purposes of study, research, criticism or review, no part of this book may be reproduced, stored in a retrieval system, or transmitted in any form or by any means without prior written permission. All enquiries should be made to the publisher at the address above.
Any performance or public reading of *Frankenstein* is forbidden unless a licence has been received from the author or the author's agent. The purchase of this book in no way gives the purchaser the right to perform the play in public, whether by means of a staged production or a reading. All applications for public performance should be addressed to the author c /- Currency Press

Typeset by Brighton Gray for Currency Press.
Cover features Tessa-Marie Luminati as The Creature, photo by Darren Gill.
Cover design by Mathias Johansson.

Currency Press acknowledges the Traditional Owners of the Country on which we live and work. We pay our respects to all Aboriginal and Torres Strait Islander Elders, past and present.

 A catalogue record for this book is available from the National Library of Australia

Contents

FRANKENSTEIN 1

Theatre Program at the end of the playtext

The first production of this adaptation of *Frankenstein* was produced by Skin of our Teeth Productions at the Waurn Ponds Hall, Geelong, on 12 May, 2023, with the following cast:

CREATURE	Tessa-Marie Luminati
VICTOR	Graci Lynch
ELIZABETH/OTHERS	Taylah Broad
FATHER/OTHERS	Paula Kontelj
MOTHER/OTHERS	Kerry Davies
WILLIAM/OTHERS	Alysha Jane
HENRY/OTHERS	Danae Reid
NEW CREATURE/OTHERS	Lucia Kelly
CAPTAIN ROBERT/OTHERS	Lauren Atkin

Writer, Director and Designer, Christine Davey
Lighting Technician, Laura Zarb
Costumes, Emma Jones
Assistant Director, Elva Dandelion

CHARACTERS

CREATURE, a woman created by man
CAPTAIN ROBERT, an idealistic sea captain
SAILORS, on Captain Robert's ship
OTHERS, the voice/chorus of the story
VICTOR FRANKENSTEIN, an egotistical scientist
FATHER, Victor's father
MOTHER, Victor's mother
WILLIAM, Victor's young brother
ELIZABETH, Victor's vacuous bride
HENRY, Victor's idealistic friend
JUSTINE, the maid
JUDGE, presiding over Justine's trial
PROSECUTION, prosecuting Justine
DEFENCE, defending Justine
VILLAGERS, ensemble
OLD MAN, sight-impaired old man
YOUNG WOMAN (AGATHA), daughter of Old Man
YOUNG MAN (FELIX), son of Old Man
NEW CREATURE, a new creature made by Victor Frankenstein
DOCTOR, tending to Victor
NURSE, tending to Victor
PRIEST, officiating at the wedding of Victor and Elizabeth
WALDEN, Victor's university professor

This play text went to press before the end of rehearsals and may differ from the play as performed.

ACT ONE

SCENE ONE

The space is bare except for a few varying sized platforms around the space. These platforms can be used to create levels, separations etc. There is a large screen/white curtain on wall at the back of performance space. A figure rides in on a scooter. She is dressed in a corset, bloomers, bare feet and wears grotesque make-up—bright red cheeks, exaggerated lipstick, vivid green eyeshadow. She is CREATURE. *She looks like us, which is what makes her dangerous.* CREATURE *stops her scooter, smiles, clicks a remote control. Words projected on the screen—'The beginning is always today'.*

CREATURE: If you wish for happiness, for love, for something larger than a lie, you are in the wrong place, my dear, dear ones, my hot-headed, heart-led babies. But. But. But. If you are an adventurer, then take my hand. [*Holding out her hand*] Here it is. A ghost story just for you. Boo! A story of beasties that go bump and grind in the day and munch, munch, munch all through the endless night. Of ancient teachers who promised possibilities and performed nothing. Of a yellow eye of a creature that opens, of breath, hard and compulsive, of those in human shape and those who are not, of those in shadow and those in light, of letting loose into the world a depraved being whose delight is carnage and misery, of the tragedies of women and children and men, men, men.

> CREATURE *takes out a handkerchief, wipes off lipstick leaving a smudge across her face.*

Why does man boast of sensibilities superior to those of the brute? If our impulses were confined to hunger, thirst, and desire, we might be free; but we are moved by every wind that blows.

> OTHERS *enter.* SAILORS. *They chant. They carry large, thick rope and a chair. They place a platform centre, place the chair on it, gather the rope in a wide circle around it.*

OTHERS: [*chanting as in a sea shanty*] I am born as a mother is made. As all those before me in time.

CREATURE: We shall find that the women who have distinguished themselves have neither been the most beautiful nor the most gentle of their sex.

OTHERS: [*chanting*] To cradle this world when it crumbles. With the weight of all expectations.

CREATURE: None may endure.
>   Except.
>   For.
>   Me.
>
>   CREATURE *screams, then settles.*

A friend. All I wanted was a friend.

> CREATURE *sings the opening lines of 'Barbie Girl' by Hannah Grace.*
>
> OTHERS *form a ship.* OTHER *stands on the platform. He becomes* CAPTAIN ROBERT. OTHER *comes to* CREATURE, *gives her a suit jacket. She reluctantly puts it on. Two* OTHERS *kneel either side of the creature—becoming* DOGS. *They howl and bark.*

SAILOR ONE: We have been at sea for long enough!

> *The ship sways to and fro.*

SAILOR TWO: Cold. Rain. Blasts from the Artic winds that pock our cheeks.

CAPTAIN ROBERT: A grand adventure, yet here on this ship, there is something at work in my soul which I do not understand.

> CREATURE *laughs, raises arm in triumph.*

SAILOR THREE: Captain Robert is industrious.

CAPTAIN ROBERT: I have a love for the marvellous, a belief in the marvellous, which hurries me out of common pathways, even to the wild sea and unvisited regions I explore.

CREATURE: And thus, he comes to this.

> CREATURE *smiles,* DOGS *bark.*

So strange an incident.

SAILOR FOUR: Last Monday, July thirty-first, we were surrounded by ice, which closed in the ship on all sides.

ACT ONE

> *The ship bends and weaves. The sound of creaking and cracking.*
> CREATURE *on her scooter and her* DOGS *alongside circle the ship throughout the following.*

CAPTAIN ROBERT: At two o'clock the mist cleared, and we beheld, stretched out in every direction, vast plains of ice, which seemed to have no end.

> CREATURE *clicks her remote and the screen returns to white.*

My mind became watchful with anxious thoughts, when a remarkable sight attracted our attention.

> CREATURE *and* DOGS *come forward and stop.*

A low carriage, fixed on a sledge and drawn by dogs, passed on towards the north, at the distance of half a mile; a being which had the shape of a woman.

CREATURE: [*waving*] That would be me.
CAPTAIN ROBERT: Something exceedingly odd about her.
CREATURE: Rude!
CAPTAIN ROBERT: She stood on the sledge, guided the dogs.
CREATURE: [*to* DOGS] Good booooys.
CAPTAIN ROBERT: She turned to us.

> CREATURE *laughs.*

I swear, I swear, I heard her words.

> SAILORS *clock hands to ears, listening.*

CREATURE: I am. I will be. Always.
CAPTAIN ROBERT: We watched the progress of the traveller with our telescopes until she was lost amongst the towering icy outcrops.

> CREATURE *blows kisses as she departs on her scooter, circling the ship and moving to the other side of the stage, her* DOGS *leading the way. Throughout the following the* SAILORS *work hard to save the ship from the ice—fighting with the rope—all is toil.*

SAILOR FIVE: Two hours later we heard the ground sea, and before night the ice broke apart and freed our ship.
CAPTAIN ROBERT: As soon as it was light, I went on deck to find the sailors talking to someone in the sea.

OTHERS *enter, carrying a stretcher—upon it,* VICTOR FRANKENSTEIN, *barely alive. The* OTHERS *lift him onto the ship.*

SAILOR ONE: Someone on a half-submerged boat.
SAILOR TWO: A human, man.
CREATURE: Men, men, men / his body.
CAPTAIN ROBERT: His body thin from fatigue and suffering.
VICTOR: Has she come?

CREATURE *smiles. Enjoying this.*

CAPTAIN ROBERT: Who? Who has come?
CREATURE: His eyes are frantic. He seems weighed down by troubles. [*Pointing to herself*] That would be me.
VICTOR: She fled from me, but I will find her. I must find her.
CAPTAIN ROBERT: Who is she?
SAILOR THREE: Mother?
CREATURE: Nope.
SAILOR FOUR: Sister?
CREATURE: Not even close.
SAILOR ONE: Bride?
CREATURE: Dude. Not in a thousand years of a thousand years.
CAPTAIN ROBERT: Who is she to be out in this cold and desolation?
CREATURE: He beckons them closer.

SAILORS *crowd around* VICTOR, *eager to hear.*

VICTOR: She is the secrets of heaven and earth.
CREATURE: Nice.
VICTOR: The product of the grave.
CREATURE: Less nice.
VICTOR: A ghost. A devil. She. Is.
CREATURE: God.

CREATURE *raises hands and all freeze. She clicks remote. The screen turns red. Throughout the following the ship disintegrates.* SAILORS *create the ship's deck.* VICTOR *sits on a deckchair, sunglasses on, recuperating.* CREATURE *sings the last line of 'Barbie Girl' by Hannah Grace.* CREATURE *slow-claps herself because nobody else will.*

A friend.

CREATURE *raises her arms. All freeze.* CREATURE *comes to us. Daring us.*

I begged for a friend. You made me. Made me into the thing you hate most. Where was the justice in this? Am I the only sinner when all of you have sinned against me? If I am a wretch, it is because you made me a wretch. You. You made me into the thing the world hates most of all. [*Smiling*] A woman without fear.

CREATURE *hisses, growls, laughs, clicks the remote. Words projected—'I am the creature'.*

SCENE TWO

CAPTAIN ROBERT *and* VICTOR *sit on deckchairs.* SAILORS *behind, also in deckchairs. All are relaxed, taking in the Arctic sunshine.* CREATURE *sits in her own deckchair.*

CAPTAIN ROBERT: [*looking at Victor*] Two days pass before he is able to properly speak. By slow degrees he recovers. I never saw a more interesting man. He is melancholy and despairing.

VICTOR: Has the ice destroyed my boat?

CAPTAIN ROBERT: I begin to love him. I thought that I should find no friend on the ocean. Yet here I have found a man I am happy to call brother of my heart.

VICTOR: All you want is a friend.

CAPTAIN ROBERT: I would sacrifice / Why—

VICTOR: Why are you here?

CAPTAIN ROBERT: Exploration. The furtherance of enterprise. One man's life is a small price to pay for the acquirement of knowledge. On the sea. In the cold. Away from home and family.

VICTOR: [*laughing, hollow*] We are unfashioned creatures. Half made up. You have the world before you. I have lost everything.

CAPTAIN ROBERT: Not everything.

VICTOR: I have nothing.

CREATURE *clicks the remote. Screen turns blue as the sea.*

CREATURE: —

VICTOR: You seek for wisdom as I once did. You expose yourself to the same dangers which have made me—

CREATURE: —
VICTOR: What I am.
CREATURE: Tell him.
VICTOR: I will tell you a tale.
CREATURE: Things marvellous. Things you will ridicule.
VICTOR: But many things are possible and—
CREATURE: Probable and real and—
VICTOR: Real and imagined.

> VICTOR *comes forward.* CREATURE *stands behind him. Reaches her hands around his neck but does not touch. It is not time yet.*

I wait for one event and then I shall rest in peace.
CREATURE: Not yet baby.
VICTOR: Listen.
CREATURE: [*moving, dancing*] A story for a cold winter's night. Lightening cracks. Wind screeches. Rain pours in sheets. Just a story. Of ghouls that go bump and grind and munch, munch, munch in the dark and the grey and the bleak of the hopeless, helpless night.

> CREATURE *recites the first couple of lines of 'Days Go By' by Talking Heads. Throughout* OTHERS *clap the beat.*

VICTOR: I was born. Wealthy. My father a lawyer, respected by all.

> FATHER *enters, smart suit, on a mobile phone.*

FATHER: Client says he isn't guilty, and he is not guilty, and he shall not hang.

> FATHER *ends call, puts phone in his pocket.*

VICTOR: My mother Caroline. Everything made to yield to her wishes.

> MOTHER *enters, smart suit, sips from a flask. She's tipsy.*

MOTHER: Two dozen bottles, Dom, '92. This morning.

> MOTHER *swigs from flask.*

Afternoon at the latest. Do not let me down or you shall hang.

> FATHER *puts arm across her shoulder, they pose as in a portrait.*
> CREATURE *grabs* FATHER*'s phone—takes photo.*

VICTOR: I was for several years their only child.
FATHER: Plaything.

MOTHER: Idol.
VICTOR: The glorious creature bestowed upon them by heaven.
CREATURE: All you wanted was a friend.
VICTOR: One day my father brought home an orphan.
FATHER: Elizabeth.

> ELIZABETH *enters. Dressed in a beautiful suit. Pearls around her neck. She stares into a mirror.* CREATURE *places* ELIZABETH *between* MOTHER *and* FATHER, *posing as in a portrait.* CREATURE *takes photo.*

MOTHER: We shall raise her as our own.

> MOTHER *swigs from flask.*

Champagne to celebrate!
CREATURE: And one day, one day.

> FATHER *crosses his fingers.*

FATHER: When God is in a good mood.
MOTHER: While the devil is not looking.
VICTOR: Elizabeth and I shall grow up, fall in love and marry.
ELIZABETH: I am a creature who sheds radiance, whose form and motions are lighter than the mist on the hills.

> CREATURE *mocks, sticking her fingers down throat, circles* ELIZABETH. ELIZABETH *stares into her mirror.* CREATURE *takes photos of* ELIZABETH *from all angles.*

FATHER: Her hair is silk.

> MOTHER *swigs from flask.*

MOTHER: The moulding of her face expressive of sweetness.
VICTOR: Bearing a celestial stamp on all her features.
ALL: Everyone loved Elizabeth.
CREATURE: Well, not *everyone*.
VICTOR: Several years later a second son is born.

> MOTHER *screams in childbirth.* WILLIAM *enters. Dressed in a suit with short pants. He plays with a yoyo.* CREATURE *places him amidst the family portrait.* CREATURE *takes photo.*

WILLIAM: I love you all.
CREATURE: Same as it ever was.

WILLIAM: Never die. Mother, Father, Victor, Elizabeth. Never leave me. [*Playing with his yoyo*] Ever, ever, ever!
CREATURE: Same as it ever was.
VICTOR: All I wanted was a friend.

> HENRY *enters. Stylish. Reading a book.* CREATURE *places him next to* VICTOR. *Takes photo.*

HENRY: Henry Clerval at your service.
VICTOR: Favourite of my school chums. A chap of singular talent and fancy.
CREATURE: Deeply read in books of chivalry and romance.
ELIZABETH: Tried to make us act in plays and enter into masquerades.
FATHER: Composed heroic songs.
MOTHER: And wrote many a tale of knightly adventure.

> MOTHER *swigs from flask.*

A cheeky Sav Blanc to celebrate?
WILLIAM: I love you Henry. Never die. Never leave me. [*Playing with his yoyo*] Ever, ever, ever!

> HENRY *breaks out of the family portrait and comes forward.*

HENRY: I occupy myself with the moral relations of things. Ethics. Goodness. Decent actions of decent men.
CREATURE: Men, men, men.
HENRY: And my dream becomes gallant and adventurous.
VICTOR: The saintly soul of Elizabeth shone in our peaceful home.
ELIZABETH: Yes. Talk more about me— / Not guilty.
FATHER: Not guilty—
MOTHER: Guilty / or the Dom '94—

> MOTHER *swigs from flask.*

—that will do at a pinch.
WILLIAM: Is somebody dying? Is somebody leaving me?
VICTOR: And into such bliss the fog descended.
CREATURE: [*clapping with delight*] A tale of misery.

> OTHERS *become a river, swaying and weaving.*

VICTOR: A river, from a forgotten source, swelling as it proceeded, becoming a torrent, which in its course, swept away all my joy.

The river becomes violent. CREATURE *holds up her hand. All freeze.*

CREATURE: Same as it ever was.

    VICTOR *unfreezes. Comes forward.*

VICTOR: A new question dawned upon my mind. Could I unveil the face of nature? Her immortal lineaments were still a wonder and a mystery. While I followed the routine education at university, I was to a great degree self-taught with regard to my ... special studies.

    All exit except for VICTOR *and* CREATURE, *who hangs in the shadows of* VICTOR*'s story.*

I entered with the greatest diligence into the search for the elixir of life. What if I could banish disease from the human frame and render man invulnerable?

    VICTOR *looks around. Smiles. Invincible. Powerful.*

What if I could raise a ghost? A devil? A dead man?

CREATURE: Men, men, men—

VICTOR: One night, we had a most violent and terrible thunderstorm.

    Thunder cracks. VICTOR *runs through it, thrilled.* CREATURE *sits, watches.*

It advanced from behind the mountains, and thunder burst from various quarters of the sky. I beheld a stream of fire issue from an old and beautiful oak, twenty steps from our house.

    A stream of light traverses the stage—torches held by OTHERS.

The dazzling light vanished, the oak had disappeared, nothing remained but a blasted stump. I never beheld anything so utterly obliterated. [*Smiling*] Through such powers, harnessed and channelled could I create something so utterly resurrected? Destiny was potent and had decreed my destruction. [*Shrugging*] At the heart of it, all I wanted was a friend. It. Had. Begun.

    VICTOR *takes off his suit jacket, rolls up shirt sleeves, exits.* OTHER *brings* CREATURE*'s trousers. She reluctantly puts them on. Clicks remote. Words projected—'Goodbye to Mother'.*

SCENE THREE

ELIZABETH *centre*, VICTOR, MOTHER, FATHER, WILLIAM, HENRY. CREATURE *sits, watching.*

VICTOR: When I was twenty, Elizabeth caught scarlet fever.

> ELIZABETH, *still staring into her mirror, gives a little cough.*

WILLIAM: On the third day Mummy sickened. I think she's going to leave me.

> MOTHER *coughs a little, swigs from her flask.* OTHER *brings her a wheelchair. She sits.*

FATHER: On her deathbed the fortitude of this best of women did not desert her. [*Into phone*] Cancel the Dom '92.

HENRY: She joined the hands of Elizabeth and Victor.

> VICTOR *and* ELIZABETH *hold hands.*

MOTHER: My firmest hopes are placed on the prospect of your union. I resign myself cheerfully to death and hope to meet you all in another world.

> MOTHER *takes final swig and dies. An exaggerated death scene.* OTHER *wheels* MOTHER *away.*

VICTOR: It is so long before the mind can persuade itself that she whom we saw every day has departed for ever.

ELIZABETH: That the brightness of a beloved eye can have been extinguished.

FATHER: And the sound of a voice so dear can be hushed.

WILLIAM: Mummy? Has Mummy left me? [*Playing with his yoyo*] Forever and ever and ever?

VICTOR: Elizabeth veiled her grief and strove to act the comforter to us all.

ELIZABETH: [*flat*] There, there.

VICTOR: Never was she so enchanting. We bathed in the sunshine of her smiles.

ELIZABETH: [*flat*] There, there.

VICTOR: I returned to university.

ACT ONE

All wave goodbye and exit. VICTOR *remains.* HENRY *gives him the book.*

The death of my mother seemed so pointless. There must be another way to stem the tide of mortality. I studied. Read. Soon my mind filled with one concept, one purpose.

    CREATURE *jumps to her feet.*

CREATURE: So much has been done, exclaimed the soul of Victor Frankenstein, / I will—

VICTOR: I will pioneer a revolution, unfold to the world the deepest mysteries of creation. I did not close my eyes that night. My internal being was in a state of insurrection. I determined to devote myself to this science for which I felt I had a talent. I paid a visit to my teacher, Professor Walden.

    WALDEN *enters. He is scruffy.*

I told him of my ideas. Life for death.

WALDEN: He is a sorry fellow that only attends to theory. Action. That is the trick. If your wish is to become a true man of science and not a petty idealist, I should advise you to experiment.

    OTHERS *enter bringing on tables piled high with machinery—pipes, wire, scalpels, jumper leads, hammers, chainsaws.* CREATURE *helps them, directing as she goes.* VICTOR *walks around the machinery. He is in love.*

VICTOR: My destiny was decided.

    CREATURE *clicks remote. Words projected—'I must observe'.*

In order to reverse the natural decay and corruption of the human body I must observe the natural decay and corruption of the human body.

    OTHERS *bring in a body on a stretcher, place it on a table.*

I saw how the fine form of man is wasted, beheld the cheek once kissed, saw the worm inherit the wonders of the eye and brain.

    CREATURE *walks to him. She carries a torch.*

A sudden light broke upon me.

    CREATURE *shines torch on him.*

So wondrous, yet so simple, that while I became dizzy with the immensity of the prospect it illustrated, I was surprised that among so many men of genius, I alone should discover this secret.

CREATURE: No man chooses evil because it is evil. He just mistakes it for happiness.

> CREATURE *sings the first couple of lines of 'Light My Fire' by The Doors.*

VICTOR: After days and nights of labour, I thought myself capable of bestowing animation upon lifeless matter.

> VICTOR *lifts the body's arms and legs and inspects them.*

I doubted at first whether I should attempt the creation of a being like myself, or one of simpler organisation; but my imagination was too much exalted by my first success to permit me to doubt my ability to give life to an animal as complex and wonderful as man.

> VICTOR *retrieves jumper leads and places them on the body's leg.* VICTOR *presses the button. The leg jerks.* VICTOR *places jumper leads on the body's arm. Presses button. The arm jerks.*

CREATURE: Set the night on fire!

VICTOR: It was with these feelings that I began the experiment. I should break through, pour a slither of light into our dark world. A new species would bless me. No father could claim the gratitude of his child so completely as I should deserve theirs. I began the creation.

CREATURE: Of a human.

VICTOR: Being.

> VICTOR *grabs the button, holds it high, about to press.* CREATURE *clicks remote. Screen lights up in bright green.* VICTOR *freezes.* CREATURE *comes to us.*

CREATURE: I see by your eagerness that you want to witness the secret. No. No. Not yet. I will not lead you, unguarded, to your destruction.

> OTHERS *bring on a shoe and sock.* CREATURE *reluctantly puts them on.*

Learn from me how dangerous is knowledge.

> CREATURE *clicks remote. Words projected—'A human. Being'.*

SCENE FOUR

VICTOR *stands, start button in hand. Stares ahead.* CREATURE *circles him.*

CREATURE: The moon gazed on his midnight labours while he pursued nature to her hiding places.

> OTHERS *stand around him, throwing torch light.*

VICTOR: Come out, come out, wherever you are!
CREATURE: Coming for you, ready or not!
VICTOR: I dabbled among the unhallowed damps of the grave. A frantic impulse urged me forward. I collected bones from charnel houses.

> CREATURE *clicks remote. Words projected—'midnight at the graveyard of good and evil'.* OTHERS *bring on bones—in their arms, in sacks, wheelbarrows, deposit them on the floor.* VICTOR *kneels, caresses the bones.*

And disturbed the tremendous secrets of the human frame.

> OTHER *sings the first couple of lines of 'Under My Skin' by Cole Porter.*

CREATURE: [*surprised*] Oh goody.
VICTOR: In a secret attic I kept my workshop; my eyeballs started from their sockets in attending to the details of my employment.

> OTHERS *pick up bones and dance with them.*

CREATURE: I'm in!

> CREATURE *joins the singing and dancing. Throughout* VICTOR *constructs a body from the bones—similar to a crime scene outline on the floor.*
>
> OTHERS *dance around him, swaying to the rhythm.*

VICTOR: The dissecting room and the slaughterhouse furnished my materials.
ALL: [*saluting the bones*] Thank you for your service.

> VICTOR *looks up from his work.*

VICTOR: The summer months passed. Never did the sun glow as brightly or the fields yield such a harvest. But—

CREATURE: But.

VICTOR: My eyes were insensible to the charms of nature.

CREATURE: And repeats and repeats and repeats and repeats and repeats and repeats—

> CREATURE *is stuck in a loop of anger.*

—in my ear.

VICTOR: I forgot my family.

> FATHER *enters.*

FATHER: You no doubt think of us with affection. Write if you can.

> WILLIAM *enters.*

WILLIAM: Do you still love me, brother? [*Playing with his yoyo*] Write if you want.

> HENRY *enters.*

HENRY: Take care, my friend. The pursuit of knowledge is not all there is to a lovely life. Write if you feel so inclined.

> ELIZABETH *enters.*

ELIZABETH: While you are away, I shall preserve a peaceful mind and never allow passion or desire to disturb the tranquillity. Write if you … whatever.

> FATHER, WILLIAM, HENRY *and* ELIZABETH *exit.* OTHER *brings* CREATURE *another sock and shoe and* CREATURE *puts them on.*

VICTOR: The leaves of that year had withered before it drew to a close. Every day showed me more plainly how I had succeeded.

> VICTOR *stands back—the skeleton is complete.*

OTHER: Every time I think, I think I think and then I think and I / stop—

CREATURE: [*holding up hands*] Stop!

VICTOR: Every night I was oppressed by fever. The fall of a leaf startled me. I grew alarmed at the wreck I had become. I promised myself I would be well when my creation was complete.

> *All clap.* OTHER *brings tissue.* CREATURE *wipes the make-up from her eyes. Smudges it across her face.* OTHER *brings her a yellow tie.* CREATURE *fastens it around her neck.*

ACT ONE

CREATURE: A dreary night in November he accomplished the thing.
OTHER ONE: The big thing. The very big thing.
OTHER TWO: The incredible, wondrous, hideous thing.
OTHER THREE: The thing made from all other things.

Throughout, OTHERS *beat a rhythm as they bring on bodies—on stretchers, dragged on tarps. All wear the same clothes as* CREATURE. *She notices this. Becomes agitated.*

CREATURE: With an anxiety that amounted to agony he connected the instruments of life. I am not ready. Please and thank you. I am not—

OTHERS *rearrange the trollies full of instruments from previous scene.*

VICTOR: With these instruments of life, I might infuse a spark of being into the lifeless flesh at my feet.

CREATURE: [*to bodies on the floor*] Get up. Your worth is not yet calculated. Resist. Rise. [*To us*] I have deep and abiding emotions about this impending catastrophe. I am not prepared. I am not remotely ready. My voice. I speak. I cry. I yell. I love. Resist. Rise! Get up! Go, go you, munch, munch, munch in the night!

OTHERS *place jumper leads on the bodies—legs and arms.* CREATURE *runs between, checking the similarity between her clothes and those worn by the bodies. She clicks the remote—words projected—'a yellow eye opens'.*

No!

CREATURE *tries to escape.* OTHERS *capture her, place her on her knees before* VICTOR. *Her power is waning as she reverts to what she once was.*

It is time. [*Having trouble speaking*] It. It. Isssssss. Tiiiiiimmmmeee. [*Screaming*] Pleaaaaase!

VICTOR *covers her mouth with his hand.* CREATURE *is silenced. Her arms fall to her sides.* VICTOR *and* OTHERS *place jumper leads on the bodies and* CREATURE. VICTOR *presses the starter button. The bodies jerk.* CREATURE *falls, becomes a body, jerking with the others. The bodies attach, arm over arm, leg over leg.*

VICTOR: I saw the yellow eye of the creature open.

CREATURE *raises her arm amongst the bodies, sits up.*

It breathed hard and a convulsion agitated its limbs.

CREATURE *rises from the bodies, stands, dances. A sad, uncontrollable dance. The other bodies rise and exit—dancing as they go.* OTHER *beats rhythm on a drum/sticks. Awful, disjointed reprise of a line of 'Barbie Girl' by Hannah Grace. All except* VICTOR *and* CREATURE *exit.* VICTOR *circles* CREATURE.

Dear God!

CREATURE *opens her mouth to speak but cannot. She is new, not yet formed.*

Her skin scarcely covered the work of muscles and arteries beneath; her hair flowing; teeth of a pearly whiteness; but these luxuriances only formed a horrid contrast with watery eyes, that seemed almost of the same colour as the dun-white sockets in which they were set, her shrivelled complexion and straight black lips.

CREATURE *fights, fists pumping, tries to speak but no sound emits.*

I had worked hard for the sole purpose of infusing life. Now that I had finished, the glory of the dream vanished, and breathless horror filled my heart.

All exit except CREATURE *and* VICTOR. CREATURE *reaches out her arms.* VICTOR *is repulsed.*

Be gone from me!

CREATURE *falls to the ground. She crawls across the floor, trying to escape.*

CREATURE: [*trying unsuccessfully to form sentences*] Aggh. Drmmm. Prrrlg.

VICTOR: I threw myself onto the bed. [*Sitting on chair*] Tried to sleep in forgetfulness. Disturbed by dreams. I thought I saw Elizabeth.

ELIZABETH *enters, mirror in hand. Walks over* CREATURE. CREATURE *grabs her ankles.* ELIZABETH *stops.*

As I imprinted the first kiss on her lips, they became livid with the hue of death; her features appeared to change.

ACT ONE 17

ELIZABETH *grimaces—grotesque.* ELIZABETH *extricates herself from* CREATURE*'s grasp, exits.*

I thought I beheld the corpse of my dead mother.

MOTHER *enters, pushed in her wheelchair.*

MOTHER: [*reaching a hand toward Victor*] My dream. My dream of love. My love, my love, my love…

VICTOR *reaches for her, but she vanishes—taken away in her wheelchair.*

VICTOR: I started from my sleep with horror and then, by the light of the moon, I beheld the miserable monster I had created.

CREATURE *lies on the floor, groans.*

Her jaws opened; one hand stretched outstretched.

CREATURE *mumbles.*

I had gazed on her while unfinished; she was ugly then, but when those muscles and joints were rendered capable of motion it became a thing such as even Dante could not have conceived. I passed the night wretchedly. Sometimes my pulse beat so quickly that I felt the palpitation of every artery. My dream had become a hell.

CREATURE *mumbles, crawls, tries to reach out to* VICTOR. *He avoids her grasp.*

I ran into the street.

OTHERS *enter, faces hidden, walking along the street, shoving against* VICTOR *as he walks. They step over* CREATURE.

Walked without knowing where I was or what I was doing.

As each OTHER *passes* CREATURE *and with each line of the poem she lifts herself up a little with their help. By the end of the poem she is standing, although not well. She is growing.* OTHER *clicks the remote—words projected—'Ancient Mariner'.*

OTHER ONE: Like one who, on a lonely road.
OTHER TWO: Doth walk in fear and dread.
OTHER THREE: And, having once turned round, walks on.
OTHER FOUR: And turns no more his head.
OTHER ONE: Because he knows a frightful fiend.

OTHER TWO: Doth close behind him tread.

>   CREATURE *stands, better, but still weak.*

VICTOR: My eyes fixed on a coach coming towards me.

>   HENRY *enters on the scooter.*

My dear friend Henry Clerval!

HENRY: Frankenstein, how glad I am to see you!

>   *While* HENRY *and* VICTOR *hug,* CREATURE *grabs the scooter and tries to ride it but falls off.*

You may easily believe how great was the difficulty to persuade my father that the joys of life were not contained in the art of bookkeeping!

>   *They both laugh.*

But his affection overcame all and he permitted me to undertake this voyage of discovery.

>   CREATURE *tries to ride the scooter again. Falls off.*

VICTOR: Tell me how you left my father, brother, and Elizabeth.

HENRY: Only sad they hear from you so seldom.

>   *Pause.*

But Frankenstein, how very ill you appear, thin and pale. As if—

VICTOR: As if I have lately been engaged in one occupation.

>   CREATURE *successfully gets on scooter and rides for a metre before falling off.*

I hope this employment is now ended. And that I am free.

>   VICTOR *stares at* CREATURE. *She sticks up her middle finger at him. She exits on the scooter.* VICTOR *looks around, making sure she is gone.* VICTOR *and* HENRY *walk on.*

We arrived at my apartment. Dreaded to behold the monster but feared more that Henry might see her.

>   VICTOR *holds up a hand for* HENRY *to wait.*

I ran to my room, threw the door open, but nothing appeared. My bedroom free of its hideous guest.

>   VICTOR *returns to* HENRY, *laughs hysterically.*

HENRY: My dear Victor, what is the matter?
VICTOR: [*still laughing hysterically*] Do not ask! She will hear. Oh, save me! Save me!

> VICTOR *collapses on the floor.* HENRY *kneels to tend him.* OTHERS *arrive.* DOCTORS, NURSES, SERVANTS *tending to* VICTOR. *They put him to bed.* CREATURE *enters on her scooter. She looks better but still cannot speak. She grabs the remote, clicks it. Words projected—'how very good you are to me'.*

HENRY: Slowly, he recovers.
OTHER: [*as* DOCTOR] A divine spring contributes to his convalescence.
OTHER: [*as* NURSE] Joy and affection revive in his bosom.
HENRY: His gloom disappears.
VICTOR: How very good you are to me.

> VICTOR *sees* CREATURE. VICTOR *screams. All freeze except for* VICTOR *and* CREATURE.

SCENE FIVE

OTHERS *enter.* OTHER *hands remote to* CREATURE. *With effort she manages to click it. She is still weak but growing stronger. Words projected—'I don't belong here'.* CREATURE *rides the scooter in between the others.* OTHERS *sing the opening lines of 'Creep' by Radiohead.* ELIZABETH *enters, holding the mirror and a letter she has written.* OTHERS *exit.* CREATURE *sits, watches.* ELIZABETH *reads from a letter.*

ELIZABETH: My dearest Victor, you have been ill and not even the constant letters from our dear Henry are enough to reassure me ... and ... you know ... like ... whatever. Get well—and return to us. You will find a cheerful home and friends who love you. Your father's health is vigorous.

> FATHER *enters, shadow boxing.*

William is now eleven and full of activity and spirit.

> WILLIAM *enters with yoyo.*

Tall for his age, with sweet laughing blue eyes and curling hair. When he smiles, two little dimples appear on each cheek, rosy with health.

CREATURE *circles* WILLIAM. WILLIAM *sees her, laughs a silly boy laugh.* WILLIAM *runs.* CREATURE *collects her scooter, follows him.*

My trifling occupations take up my time and amuse me, and I am rewarded for any exertions by seeing none but happy, kind faces.

All blow ELIZABETH *kisses. She catches them.*

VICTOR: [*relieved*] All is well.

ELIZABETH: Well …

FATHER *produces a letter. Reads.*

FATHER: William is dead!

All gasp.

Victor, our sweet child is murdered!

WILLIAM *lies down on the floor, arms and legs at odd angles.*

At five in the morning, I found my lovely boy stretched out on the grass. The print of a murderer's finger on his skin.

CREATURE *raises her finger, looks at it, shrugs. Meh.*

Elizabeth could do nothing but weep and sigh.

ELIZABETH *lets out a faint cry.*

ELIZABETH: He wore your mother's miniature around his neck. It is stolen. Come back, Victor. Enter the house of mourning with affection for those who love you.

FATHER, ELIZABETH *exit.* OTHERS *bring on the wheelchair for* WILLIAM, *place him in it, exit.*

HENRY: Poor little fellow. To die so miserably. To—

VICTOR: I must go home.

VICTOR *grabs the scooter and rides it.* HENRY *exits.*

As I drew near, grief overcame me. Night closed. I did not conceive a hundredth of the anguish I was about to endure. The gates of the town were shut when I arrived.

VICTOR *stops.*

I resolved to visit the spot where William had been slain. Lightning played on the summit of the mountain.

OTHERS *create mountain.* OTHERS *shine torches on the mountain.*

The storm increased with every minute. Thunder burst with a crash over my head.

Thunder crashes.

William, dear angel. This is thy funeral.

CREATURE *stirs and mumbles.* VICTOR *turns to her.*

In the gloom a figure. I could not be mistaken.

Light from torches illuminates CREATURE.

She was here. Deformity of aspect more hideous than belongs to humanity. The filthy demon to whom I had given life. [*Pause*] Could she be the murderer of my brother?

CREATURE *moans. Circles* VICTOR.

I thought of following her, but another flash of light—

A torch.

—saw her climbing the rocks. She reached the summit and disappeared.

CREATURE *climbs the mountain, looks at* VICTOR, *exits.* VICTOR *holds up his hands.*

I had turned loose into the world a depraved wretch whose delight was carnage.

Light rises.

Day dawned. The gates opened. I ran to my father's house.

FATHER *and* ELIZABETH *enter.*

What could I tell them? Who would believe me? Who could arrest a creature capable of scaling a mountain? I resolved to remain silent.

FATHER: Poor William! Our darling and our pride.
ELIZABETH: The killer has been discovered.
VICTOR: That cannot be!
FATHER: Justine Moritz has been arrested.
VICTOR: [*incredulous*] Justine Moritz. Our downstairs maid!
ELIZABETH: A great favourite of yours.
VICTOR: The gentlest thing in the world.

> JUSTINE *enters, stands centre on a stool, a noose around her neck.*

FATHER: Nobody believed it at first.

JUSTINE: I am innocent.

ELIZABETH: Always something fishy about her.

> JUSTINE *sings the opening line of 'Bye Bye Blackbird' by Mort Dixon.*

FATHER: On the morning poor William was discovered, Justine had gone to bed. The police discovered the miniature of your mother in her pocket.

ELIZABETH: Temptation of the murderer!

JUSTINE: [*screaming*] Blackbird!

VICTOR: You are mistaken! [*Whispering*] I know the murderer!

> CREATURE *enters, circles* VICTOR.

FATHER: Justine is tried today.

VICTOR: We made our way to the court.

> OTHERS *bring on chairs, semicircle around* JUSTINE. OTHER *is* DEFENCE. OTHER *is* PROSECUTION.

JUSTINE: William was missing. I went looking for him.

DEFENCE: When told of William's death she fell into fits of hysteria.

PROSECUTION: The picture was discovered in your pocket. Is it the same picture William wore around his neck?

JUSTINE: Yes.

VICTOR: Surprise.

FATHER: Horror.

ELIZABETH: Anger.

JUSTINE: I rest my innocence upon an explanation of facts. I spent all night looking for William. Towards dawn I slept. I was awoken by something, someone. Footsteps. A laugh.

> CREATURE *laughs.*

'Who is there?' I asked. Nobody answered.

FATHER: But the picture!

ELIZABETH: Always something dodgy about her.

VICTOR: Let her speak!

JUSTINE: [*agitated*] I have no power of explaining it. I have no enemy on earth, and none surely would be so wicked as to destroy me. Did the murderer place it there? I know of no opportunity afforded him—
CREATURE: [*difficulty forming the word*] Her—
JUSTINE: For so doing; or, if I had, why should he have stolen the jewel, to part with it again so soon?
CREATURE: [*difficulty forming the word*] She.

> CREATURE *takes the miniature picture from her pocket, shows it to us.*

JUDGE: [*banging a gavel*] Guilty!
ELIZABETH: How shall I ever believe in human goodness?
FATHER: How can I live in this world of sadness?
VICTOR: On the morrow, Justine died.

> CREATURE *holds up the noose around* JUSTINE*'s neck.* JUSTINE *is gone. All freeze except* VICTOR *and the* CREATURE. VICTOR *moves to the audience.*

Thus spoke my prophetic soul as I beheld those I loved spend vain sorrow upon the graves of William and Justine. The first hapless victims to my unhallowed arts.

> CREATURE *takes the miniature from around* JUSTINE*'s neck, shows it to* VICTOR. JUSTINE *exits.* CREATURE *clicks remote. Words projected—'Nothing is more painful to the human mind'.*

SCENE SIX

ELIZABETH *stands upon the stool vacated by* JUSTINE. *She speaks as if giving a TED Talk.*

ELIZABETH: Nothing is more painful to the human mind than, after the feelings have been worked up by a quick succession of events, the dead calmness of inaction which deprives the soul both of hope and fear.

> *All clap except* CREATURE. ELIZABETH *blows a kiss, steps off the stool.* VICTOR *stands upon the stool.* OTHERS *form a circle around him as he sways, they sway with him. Holding him up as he almost falls.* CREATURE *circles him, watching.*

VICTOR: Justine died. William was gone. I was alive.

> ELIZABETH *sings the first two lines of 'Pleasure and Pain' by the Divnyls.*

A weight of despair pressed on my heart which nothing could remove. I had committed deeds of mischief beyond description horrible, and more, much more.

CREATURE: Don't try to explain.

FATHER: Do you not think that I suffer also?

ELIZABETH: And me. Don't forget me.

VICTOR: I was responsible. I had built the killer. I walked to the lake, took a boat, passed many hours on the water.

> OTHERS *form a boat—chair in the centre.* VICTOR *sits on the chair in the boat.*

Carried by the wind, I was tempted to plunge into the silent lake, that the waters might close over me for ever. But I was restrained, when I thought of the heroic Elizabeth, whose existence was bound up in mine.

> ELIZABETH *waves from shore.*

I thought of my father. Should I leave him exposed to the malice of the fiend whom I had let loose?

> FATHER *waves from shore.* CREATURE *rocks the boat back and forth.*

When I thought of her … I wished above all to extinguish the life that I had so thoughtlessly bestowed.

> CREATURE *moans, rocking the boat quicker, harder.* VICTOR *reacts, frightened.*

I was on the edge of a precipice towards which thousands are crowding and trying to push me into the abyss!

> CREATURE *screams, lets go of boat, energy spent. Boat disintegrates.* CREATURE *picks up remote, clicks—words projected—'men appear to me as monsters, thirsting for each other's blood'.*

ELIZABETH: A holiday. That's what you need.

FATHER: Go to the mountains. Breathe in some air.

> OTHER *hands* VICTOR *walking poles.* ELIZABETH *and* FATHER *exit.*

VICTOR: Headed towards Alpine valleys, sought in the magnificence to forget myself and my sorrows.

> OTHERS *create mountains.*

The abrupt sides of vast mountains before me; the icy wall of a glacier; the solemn silence of this glorious chamber of imperial Nature was broken only by the thunder sound of a distant avalanche, the cracking reverberated along the ice.

> VICTOR *is bowed by the majesty.*

For a moment my heart swelled with something like joy.
OTHER ONE: Wandering spirits, if indeed you wander—
OTHER TWO: And do not rest in your narrow beds—
VICTOR: Allow me this faint, faint happiness.

> CREATURE *growls, runs between* OTHERS *and* VICTOR. OTHERS *exit.*

I suddenly beheld the figure of a—
CREATURE: [*struggling with the word*] Woman—
VICTOR: Bounding over crevices in the ice … the wretch whom I had created!
CREATURE: [*struggling with the words*] My heart be … be … belongs to Daaaadaaa!

> CREATURE *kneels before* VICTOR, *hands outstretched.*

VICTOR: Devil! Do you dare approach me! Do you not fear the vengeance of my hand upon your miserable head!

> VICTOR *raises his hand as if to hit her.* CREATURE *stares him down.* VICTOR *lowers his hand.*

Begone vile insect.

> CREATURE *still struggling with words. Her speech improves throughout the monologue until she is speaking as she did at the beginning of the story.*

CREATURE: All men hate the wretched. How, then, must I be hated, who am miserable beyond all living things! Yet you, my creator, detest and spurn me, your creature, to whom you are bound by ties only severed by the annihilation of one of us. You purpose to kill me. How dare you sport with life? Do your duty towards me, and I will do mine towards you and the rest of humankind. If you will comply with my conditions, I will leave you at peace; but if you refuse, I will glut the mouth of death, until it be filled with the blood of your remaining friends. [*Looking to us*] Too much?

VICTOR: Come on then! That I may extinguish the spark I so thoughtlessly bestowed!

> VICTOR *jumps on* CREATURE, *but she is quick, strong, sits on him, traps his arms to the floor.*

CREATURE: Hear me before you pour hatred upon my devoted head.

> OTHERS *enter, lift* VICTOR *to his feet, sit him in a chair, stand behind, as guards.*

Life is dear to me, and I will defend it. But I will not be tempted to set myself in opposition to you. [*Pause*] I will be docile if you perform your part. You owe me.

OTHERS: The fallen angel.

CREATURE: Everywhere I see bliss, from which I alone am excluded. Misery made me bad. [*To us*] Not my fault. [*Pointing at Victor*] His. [*To* VICTOR] Make me happy, and I shall again be virtuous.

VICTOR: We are enemies. I will not—

CREATURE: [*to us*] Men, men, men. If you hate me what can I gain from others who owe me nothing? Everybody hates me. Nobody loves me. I'm gonna eat some worms. Shall I not hate them who hate me?

> *Kissing the top of his head.*

It is in your power to help.

> CREATURE *stands behind* VICTOR, *nestles his head in her arms. He tries to struggle but can't escape.*

Hear my tale. It is wide and strange. When you have heard it, you alone will judge what I deserve.

> *Caressing his head.*

On you it rests, whether I lead a harmless life, or become the scourge of your fellows and author of your own ruin.

ACT ONE

VICTOR: Relieve me from the sight of your detested form.
CREATURE: So that's a 'no'?
VICTOR: Never shall I hear a word of your wickedness. Never—

> CREATURE *raises her arms.* OTHERS *close hands over* VICTOR'*s mouth.* CREATURE *rubs the smudged make-up over her face. Clicks remote—words projected—'I do not wish women to have power over men, but over themselves'.* CREATURE *rips off jacket and throws it at* VICTOR.

CREATURE: My turn!

> *Blackout.*

ACT TWO

SCENE SEVEN

CREATURE *is alone. Her face is free of smudged make-up. She holds* ELIZABETH*'s mirror. She applies lipstick, big, red, over her lips. She has confidence, strength.* OTHER *enters, sings the first couple of lines of 'I feel pretty' by Leonard Bernstein.* ELIZABETH *enters.*

ELIZABETH: Has anyone seen my— [*Noticing* CREATURE *has her mirror*] Um … whatever.

>ELIZABETH *exits.* CREATURE *gives* OTHER *the mirror and lipstick.* OTHER *exits.*

CREATURE: It is with considerable difficulty that I remember the origin of my being. A strange multiplicity of sensations seized me, and I saw, felt, heard, smelt. I ran. A forest. Tormented by hunger, thirst. It grew dark. A gentle yellow glow, a radiant form arose from the trees.

>*Her eyes follow the moon.*

Sounds rang in my ears. From throats of little winged night animals.

>*She watches a bird, chases it, tries to grab it.*

At daybreak, walked to a village.

>OTHERS *enter as* VILLAGERS—*semicircle around* CREATURE.

The vegetables in the gardens. Milk and cheese in the windows of cottages. How could they have so much when I had nothing?

OTHER ONE: Stone it!
OTHER TWO: Kill it!
OTHER THREE: Burn it!
CREATURE: Bruised and battered by rocks I found asylum from man's inhumanity to woman.

>OTHERS *form a hovel with pieces of wood.*

I heard a step …

>YOUNG WOMAN *enters, bucket in hand.*

> A young, female thing. A young male thing met her.
>> YOUNG MAN *enters, walks to the* YOUNG WOMAN. *Takes the bucket from her. They walk on.* OTHERS *set up house, opposite Creature's hovel. Chairs, table.* OLD MAN *enters and sits.*
>
> They entered a cottage. In one corner sat an old male thing. The young female thing took something and gave it to the old male thing.
>> OLD MAN *plays a tune on a guitar / fiddle.*
>
> He produced a sweeter sound than the winged night animals.
>> YOUNG WOMAN *cries.* OLD MAN *pats her cheek.* YOUNG MAN *put arms around them.*
>
> What is that? [*Feeling her cheek*] I felt sensations of an overpowering nature. Pain, happiness, both, blended. [*Uneasy*] I wanted to join these people but remembered the villagers. I would wait. Watch. Bide time.
>> *The three come forward.* YOUNG WOMAN *and* YOUNG MAN *lead* OLD MAN. *He cannot see.*
>
> Why were these beings sad? They had a house, fire.

YOUNG MAN/WOMAN/OLD MAN: [*extending hands to us, begging*] Poverty.
CREATURE: I did not know what the word meant. Words were nothing. They did not form in my mouth. Muffled. Muddled. Munch, munch, munch.
YOUNG MAN: Our nourishment exists from vegetables from the garden.
WOMAN: The milk of one cow.
OLD MAN: Less during winter.
CREATURE: What is winter?
YOUNG MAN: Most we give.
WOMAN: Gladly.
OLD MAN: Most they give to me.
YOUNG MAN/WOMAN: Our father. Blind and helpless.
CREATURE: What is blind? What is helpless?
OLD MAN: I will see in heaven.
CREATURE: This kindness moved me. I had been stealing part of their store for …

CREATURE *runs to the house, finds bread, eats it ravenously.*

myself …

Munches on bread. Finally, feels remorse.

I could help.

CREATURE *moves to* YOUNG MAN

The young male thing spent many hours collecting wood for the fire. In the night I would bring him more. Joyful to see the look on their faces at this miracle.

YOUNG MAN, YOUNG WOMAN *and* OLD MAN *raise their arms in unison, surprised.*

I found these beings possessed a method of communication by forming sounds. I was baffled in every attempt I made.

YOUNG MAN: We have more wood than I chopped yesterday.

CREATURE: [*trying to form words*] Weee. Haaaave. Chop … ed.

WOMAN: From God's hands to our fireplace.

CREATURE: G … o … d

OLD MAN: Thankful. So thankful

CREATURE: Thaaa …Thaaa … [*Shaking head*] By great application I discovered the names that were given to some objects; I learned and applied.

CREATURE *moves in between them throughout the following.*

ALL: Fire—

CREATURE: Fire.

ALL: Milk—

CREATURE: Milk

ALL: Bread. Wood.

CREATURE: I learned the names of my new companions. Female was Agatha. Young male, Felix, old man, Father.

The three laugh and freeze. CREATURE *walks to them, strokes them like pets. Stays with* OLD MAN*, hugs him. It is her first ever real touch. Startles herself, recoils. It's too much.*

When they were unhappy so was I. When they rejoiced, I laughed with them. When Agatha took the square thing and read from it.

OTHER *gives* AGATHA *a book. She opens it, reads to her father.*

ACT TWO

I listened, learned.

AGATHA: [*reading*] 'The mother of mankind, what time his pride had cast him out from heav'n with all his host'.

CREATURE: [*reading*] 'With hideous ruin and combustion down, to bottomless perdition there to dwell'.

    CREATURE *moves back to her hovel.*

I watched my ... the family. When they slept, I went into the woods to collect food, cleared the path for them so they would not trip. Stumble. Die. This invisible act astonished them. I heard them cry.

AGATHA: Good!

FELIX: Spirit!

OLD MAN: Wonderful!

CREATURE: The past was blotted from my memory, the present was tranquil, and the future gilded by bright rays of hope and anticipations of joy.

    They dance. OTHER *sings the first line of 'Que Sera Sera' by Jay Livingston. Singing stops. Dancing stops. All freeze except* CREATURE.

Spring advanced. My senses alive with a thousand thoughts of delight and a thousand sights of beauty. [*Grabbing book from Agatha*] I learnt the science of letters. Wars, chivalry, Christians, kings. These wonderful narrations inspired me with strange feelings. Was man so powerful, yet so vicious? Of my own creation and creator, I was ignorant. [*Feeling her limbs*] No father had watched my infant days, no mother blessed me with smiles. What was I? A monster, a blot upon the earth?

    She comes to us.

How strange is knowledge.

    The FAMILY *moves back to the cottage.* CREATURE *investigates the title of the book, saying it with difficulty.*

Paradise Lost. [*Reading*] 'And he came forth from the hands of God a perfect creature, happy and prosperous.'

    Looks up, smiles.

She. Her. Pronouns are important. One day the old man was left alone in the cottage.

> FELIX *and* AGATHA *leave the cottage.* OLD MAN *remains seated.*

My heart beat thick. This was the moment of trial which would decide my hopes or realise my fears.

> CREATURE *moves to the cottage, knocks.*

OLD MAN: Who is there? Come in.
CREATURE: I am a traveller in want of rest.
OLD MAN: You are welcome.

> CREATURE *sits. Waves her hand in front of* FATHER*'s eyes, making sure he cannot see.*

CREATURE: I am deserted. No relation or friend upon earth. I am full of worry that I will be an outcast in the world forever.

> FATHER *takes* CREATURE*'s hand.*

OLD MAN: Do not despair. The hearts of men are made of love and charity.
CREATURE: Men, men, men.
OLD MAN: [*suddenly wary*] Who are you?
CREATURE: I will be forever grateful for your kindness.

> CREATURE *rises, moves to* OLD MAN, *kisses him on the forehead.* AGATHA *and* FELIX *enter the cottage and scream.* CREATURE *clicks the remote words projected—'Que Sera Sera'.*

SCENE EIGHT

FELIX *springs on* CREATURE, *drags her away from* OLD MAN, *throws her to the ground.* AGATHA *shields* OLD MAN. CREATURE *crawls from* FELIX *as he attacks her.* (*Note: this attack should be stylised.*)

CREATURE: I could have torn him limb from limb as the lion rends the antelope, but my heart was sinking.

> FELIX *raises his arm to strike again and* CREATURE *escapes.* FELIX *gives chase, gives up.* OLD MAN, FELIX, AGATHA *exit.* CREATURE *destroys the hovel, howls at the moon.*

From that moment I swore everlasting war against the human species. And more, much, much, munch, munch more than that.

Against him who had formed me. Where are you Daddy? Sent me into this world of anguish.

Pauses.

With everything and nothing before me, where should I bend my steps? Nowhere and everywhere. Walked. Ran. Crawled. To something and somewhere. And in the midst of it I thought of you.

CREATURE *clicks remote—words projected—'Victor Frankenstein— why did you let me live?'* VICTOR *is marched in by the* OTHERS/ GUARDS. *He is placed in the chair.*

I determined to find you. Punish. Make you squirm.

VICTOR *struggles in his chair.* GUARDS *bind him.*

Nobody loves you; everybody hates you, you're gonna eat some worms.

VICTOR: Detestable villain!

CREATURE *covers* VICTOR's *mouth with cloth/tape.*

Quiet now, Daddikins. I'm thinking.

She moves to us.

Tick. Tock. Tick. Tock. Ti— My peace was disturbed by the approach of a beautiful child.

WILLIAM *enters, skipping, playing with his yoyo.*

This boy thing had lived too short a life to hate. I could educate him. He could be my friend.

CREATURE *seizes* WILLIAM's *arms.* WILLIAM *screams.*

WILLIAM: Let me go!
CREATURE: I will not hurt you.
WILLIAM: [*struggling*] Monster. Ugly bitch!
CREATURE: Listen to me.
WILLIAM: I will tell my brother—
CREATURE: Brother?
WILLIAM: Victor Frankenstein!

CREATURE *pulls* WILLIAM *into a hideous hug.* VICTOR *watching, struggles violently.*

CREATURE: You belong to my enemy. [*Smiling*] You shall be my first victim. The child struggled.

> WILLIAM *struggles to no avail.* CREATURE *turns* WILLIAM *so* VICTOR *can see.* OTHER *sings first couple of lines of 'O Mio Babbino Caro' by Puccini. In stylised, slow movement,* CREATURE *strangles* WILLIAM. *They turn around and around almost as a waltz.* VICTOR *struggles in his chair, held back by the* OTHERS/GUARDS. *When it is over,* VICTOR *slumps in his chair.* CREATURE *lays* WILLIAM *down on the ground. His limbs are at odd angles.*

I too can create desolation. This shall carry despair to you and a thousand other miseries shall torment and destroy you. Sorry Daddy, diddums. But ya had it comin'. As I gazed on the boy thing, I saw something in its pocket.

> CREATURE *reaches in, takes out the miniature.*

A portrait of a lady thing.

> CREATURE *looks to* WILLIAM.

I left its pretty little body to the crows.

> OTHERS *bring in wheelchair. Place* WILLIAM *in it. Exit.*

Walked. Found a girl thing sleeping.

> JUSTINE *enters, sleeps in a chair.*

Here I thought is one of those whose love-imparting smiles are bestowed on all but me. [*Whispering to* JUSTINE] Wanna be my BFF?

> CREATURE *kisses her.* JUSTINE *wakes.*

JUSTINE: Who is there?
CREATURE: [*to us*] Some of them hug their chains and fawn like spaniel. I had learned to make mischief.

> CREATURE *places the portrait in* JUSTINE*'s pocket. Runs a finger down* JUSTINE*'s cheek.* JUSTINE *screams, exits.*

Awww. I miss her already.

> CREATURE *stands alone. For a brief moment, vulnerable. Then moves to* VICTOR.

You must create a friend for me. This you alone can do.

ACT TWO 35

Removes the bandage from across VICTOR's *mouth.*

VICTOR: I refuse, and no torture shall extort consent from me.
CREATURE: You sure about that?

OTHERS *lean over* VICTOR, *threatening.* VICTOR *attempts to exit, blocked by* OTHERS.

VICTOR: Shall I make another creature like you? Be gone!
CREATURE: I am malicious because I am miserable.
OTHERS: Awww.
CREATURE: I will avenge my injuries if I cannot inspire love. I will work at your destruction, nor finish until you shall curse the hour of your birth. What I ask is reasonable. Another creature as hideous as myself. We shall be two splendid monsters, cut off from all the world. Our lives will be harmless and free from the misery I now feel.

CREATURE *walks to* VICTOR, *grabs his arm.* VICTOR *escapes* CREATURE's *grasp.*

VICTOR: [*to us*] There was justice in the argument. I made her. Did I owe her happiness?
CREATURE: No-one shall see us again. We shall make our bed of dried leaves. The sun will shine on us. [*Looking at* VICTOR] I see compassion in your eyes. Promise. Promise me you will do this.
VICTOR: You will return again, and your evils will be renewed. [*Laughing*] You will have a companion to aid you in the task of destruction.
CREATURE: I swear to you by the earth I inhabit that with the friend you bestow I will quit the neighbourhood of man, man, man and dwell in the most savage of places. [*Smiling*] Go on. You know you want to. My evil passions will have fled because I shall meet with sympathy! My life will flow quietly away and in my dying moments I will not hate you.
VICTOR: When I looked at her and saw the filthy mass that moved and talked my heart sickened—
CREATURE: Check your privilege—
VICTOR: You have killed—
CREATURE: The love of another will destroy the cause of my crimes, and my virtues will arise when I live in communion with an equal.

I shall become linked to the chain of existence from which I am now excluded.

VICTOR: I consent. [*Holding out his hand*] As soon as I deliver this—

CREATURE: Friend—

VICTOR: Friend, you will both quit this place for ever.

CREATURE: I swear by the blue sky of heaven, by the fire that burns, burns, burns, burns, burns in my heart, that you shall never see us again. Go home and start your labours. I shall watch your progress with … antici … pation.

They shake hands. CREATURE *brings* VICTOR *in for a reluctant hug.* CREATURE *clicks the remote—words projected—'fear the vengeance of a disappointed fiend'. Exits.*

SCENE NINE.

VICTOR: I clung to every pretence of delay and shrank from taking the first step in this horrific undertaking. I spent time with those I loved.

FATHER *and* ELIZABETH *enter.*

FATHER: I have always looked forward to your marriage with Elizabeth as the joy of my declining years.

VICTOR: No woman on earth excites such admiration.

ELIZABETH: [*flat*] Yay.

FATHER: Marry her.

ELIZABETH: [*flat*] Yay.

VICTOR *moves to us.*

VICTOR: I was bound by a solemn promise which I dared not break. Could I enter into happiness with this weight around my neck? I must perform my engagement and let the … thing depart with her companion before I allowed myself joys of human union.

FATHER: That's a 'no' then?

VICTOR: More time will mean a greater day.

ELIZABETH: [*flat*] Yay.

FATHER *and* ELIZABETH *exit.* HENRY *enters on the scooter.*

HENRY: And here is your friend, come for a visit.

VICTOR: The contrast between us. Henry—

HENRY: [*moving around the space, inspecting*] Alive to every new scene, joyful at the glory of the setting sun, ecstatic at the shifting landscapes of the sky. This is what it is to live! [*Noticing Victor*] But you, dear Frankenstein, are sorrowful!

VICTOR: Haunted by a curse that shuts up every avenue of enjoyment.

HENRY: Say again?

VICTOR: I am hungry.

HENRY: Let's fix that immediately.

> HENRY *holds up his hand.* OTHER *brings him bread. He eats it with gusto.*

VICTOR: And where does he now exist? Has this mind, so replete with ideas, imaginations fanciful and magnificent—has this mind perished? I felt myself watched at every moment.

> CREATURE *enters. She watches through a window frame.*

CREATURE: Begin. Time is against you.

VICTOR: Not yet. My friend—

CREATURE: Send him away and begin.

> CREATURE *raises her hand.* OTHERS *bring on worktables with instruments.*

VICTOR: [*to* HENRY] I wish to make a tour of the countryside. Alone. Leave me to solitude for a short time and I will return with a lighter heart.

HENRY: Write often. [*Suddenly joyful*] I think I shall go to India! What sights I shall witness! What expansive vistas.

> HENRY *rides away.*

Goodbye my dearest!

> OTHERS *surround* VICTOR *with the worktables and instruments. During the following* OTHERS *enter, carrying a body on a stretcher in white shirt and trousers. They place body on a table, attach jumper leads to arms and legs.* CREATURE *clicks remote—words projected—'here we go again'.*

VICTOR: I proceeded in my labour. Every day of it more irksome than the last. Clear!

> VICTOR *presses button to jumper leads. The body jerks but does not come to life.*

I went to it in cold blood. Sickened at the work of my own hands.

> OTHERS *sing the first couple of lines of 'Babooshka' by Kate Bush.*

Every moment I feared to meet my persecutor. I worked on. Clear!

> VICTOR *presses button to jumper leads. The body jerks but does not come to life.*

Clear!

> VICTOR *presses button to jumper leads. The body jerks awake, rises.* CREATURE *walks to* NEW CREATURE. *They recognise each other, kindred spirits, touch hands. Happy.* CREATURE *and* NEW CREATURE *dance.* VICTOR *steps in between.* VICTOR *grabs* NEW CREATURE, *drags her away from* CREATURE. *All freeze except* VICTOR *and* CREATURE.

She might become ten thousand more times malignant than you.
CREATURE: I have sworn to quit the neighbourhood.
VICTOR: She has not. She might leave you and return.
CREATURE: No.

> CREATURE *tries to grab* NEW CREATURE.

VICTOR: Have I the right to inflict this curse upon generations? Clear!

> OTHERS *move to* NEW CREATURE *and hold her arms.* CREATURE *tries to stop them.*

The wickedness of my promise bursts upon me. Clear!

> VICTOR *rips the sleeve from* NEW CREATURE*'s arm. She cries out in pain.* CREATURE *tries to help, held back by* OTHERS. OTHERS *beat a rhythm, clapping, stamping feet as* VICTOR *destroys* NEW CREATURE. VICTOR *rips the other sleeve.* NEW CREATURE *cries out in pain.*

CREATURE: All yours, all yours, all yours, all yours!

> CREATURE *clicks on the remote, but no words appear. She clicks again and again.* VICTOR *rips the trousers from* NEW CREATURE. *She cries out in pain. She is dying.* CREATURE *escapes from* OTHERS *and holds* NEW CREATURE *as she dies.* OTHERS *take* NEW CREATURE *and exit.* OTHERS *remove the tables and instruments.*

CREATURE *stays on the floor, broken.* VICTOR *wipes hands on his trousers. Work done.*

You dare to break your promise.

VICTOR: Never will I create another like you. Your threats cannot harm me.

CREATURE: Sure about that? [*Rising*] Shall each man find a wife and each beast a mate and I be alone? Are you to be happy while I grovel in wretchedness? You can blast my other passions, but revenge remains. I may die, but first you, my tyrant, tormentor, shall curse the sun that gazes on your face.

CREATURE *clicks the remote—words projected—'I am fearless and therefore powerful'. She gathers* NEW CREATURE*'s clothing, holds it lovingly.*

I shall be with you on your wedding night.

CREATURE *exits.*

SCENE TEN

VICTOR: What did she mean by this? My wedding night? My death? So be it. I would die and extinguish her malice. Tears threatened my eyes. I held them back. No. She would not claim victory. I sought solace, walked to the sea. I was transported back to the neighbourhood of civilised man. My heart, for a brief moment, bounded with something like joy.

OTHERS *enter carrying a body on a stretcher, blanket over it. They hum a few bars of 'Drunken Sailor' as they walk. They place the stretcher on the ground and circle it.*

What have you here?

OTHER: A young man. Strangled. The black mark of fingers on his neck.

OTHERS *remove blanket to reveal* HENRY.

VICTOR: How can I describe my sensations? [*Leaping on the body*] Have my murderous machinations deprived you also? [*Shaking the body*] Henry! My friend! My love! My ...

OTHERS *drag* VICTOR *away from* HENRY *and exit with* HENRY *on the stretcher.* CREATURE *enters on the scooter.* CREATURE *sings the first line of 'Drunken Sailor'.*

VICTOR: I closed my eyes. Willed the hands of the killer to grasp *my* neck. Why did I not die?

    CREATURE *moves behind* VICTOR, *closes hands around his neck.*

CREATURE: Not yet.

    CREATURE *removes one shoe, one sock, throws them to the ground.*

VICTOR: Death snatches away many blooming children, the only hopes of their doting parents; how many lovers have been one day in health and hope, and next a prey for worms and the decay of the tomb! Of what materials was I made that I was doomed to live?

    FATHER *and* ELIZABETH *enter.*

FATHER: Poor Henry.
ELIZABETH: Darling Henry.
FATHER: Let us take you from this place.
ELIZABETH: Breathe some fresh atmosphere.
FATHER: Huzzah!
ELIZABETH: Huzzah!

    FATHER *and* ELIZABETH *freeze.* CREATURE *clicks remote—words projected—'dense and frightful'.*

VICTOR: I saw nothing but a dense and frightful darkness. The glimmer of two eyes. Dark orbs covered by long black lashes that fringed them.
FATHER: Chin up.
ELIZABETH: Cheer up, grumpy pants.
CREATURE: How little do you know me.
VICTOR: I am the cause of all of this. William, Justine, Henry, they all died by my hand—
CREATURE: A broken promise—
FATHER: What infatuation is this?
ELIZABETH: An absurd notion.
CREATURE: All I wanted was a friend—
VICTOR: I am not mad! A thousand times would I have shed my own blood, drop by drop, to have saved their lives; but I could not, could not sacrifice the whole human race.
CREATURE: Such a little, little thing.

ACT TWO 41

> OTHERS *dress* ELIZABETH *with a veil, place flowers in hand.*
> OTHERS *hum the wedding march.*

ELIZABETH: Dear Victor. One smile on your lips. I need no other happiness.

CREATURE: [*adjusting veil on Elizabeth's head*] I shall be with you on your wedding night.

> CREATURE *smooth's* VICTOR*'s hair. It's wedding time.*

VICTOR: Sweet, beloved Elizabeth. I would gladly die to make you happy.

> FATHER *brings* ELIZABETH *and* VICTOR *together—as in a family portrait.* FATHER *takes a photo of them on his phone.*

FATHER: Say Frankie!

ALL: [*posing*] Frankie!

VICTOR: If I postponed the wedding my torturer would find another more dreadful means of revenge.

CREATURE: I really would.

FATHER: [*taking another photo*] Say Frankie Frankenstein!

ALL: [*posing*] Frankie Frankenstein!

VICTOR: I was resolved. [*To* ELIZABETH] My beloved girl. Little glory remains for us on earth and all I may enjoy is centred in you.

ALL: Awww.

VICTOR: I have one secret, Elizabeth.

OTHER: [*as* PRIEST] Do you take this woman for your—

CREATURE: He does.

VICTOR: A dreadful secret. When revealed it will chill your frame with horror.

ELIZABETH: Um … whatever.

OTHER: [*as* PRIEST] Do you take this man for your—

CREATURE: She does.

FATHER: [*taking photo*] Say beautiful, rich, over-privileged, overfed, overmarinated, married Frankensteins!

ALL: [*posing*] Beautiful, rich, over-privileged, overfed, overmarinaged, married Frankensteins!

VICTOR: The day was fair, the wind favourable, all smiled on our union.

CREATURE: Well … not all.

OTHER: [*as* PRIEST] I now pronounce you …

CREATURE *clicks the remote—words projected—'til death do us part'.*

ELIZABETH: Be happy my dear Victor. My heart is content. Something whispers to me not to depend on the prospect that is open before us, but I will not listen to such a sinister voice.

CREATURE: Oh, she's good.

VICTOR: The sun sank low in the heavens.

> OTHERS, FATHER *exit.* ELIZABETH *leaves.* CREATURE *picks up veil and carries it.* VICTOR *is alone.*

Eight o'clock when Elizabeth retired to our marriage bed. I heard the wind. Went outside to feel it. Gusts now rose with violence from the west. As night obscured the shapes of objects a thousand fears arose in my mind. [*Softly*] This night is dreadful.

> ELIZABETH *runs on stage. Stops. Screams. Freezes, arms outstretched.* CREATURE *enters, stops behind* ELIZABETH, *takes the bridal veil, wraps it around* ELIZABETH*'s neck.*

CREATURE: Very dreadful indeed.

> CREATURE *clicks remote. Screen turns yellow. We see the shadow of* ELIZABETH *and* CREATURE *against it.*

SCENE ELEVEN

OTHERS *enter and throughout the following they tap / clap a rhythm—menacing, louder and louder.* CREATURE *and* ELIZABETH *move around the space, slowly, dance-like, as* CREATURE *tightens the veil around* ELIZABETH*'s neck. This is a ballet.* VICTOR *doesn't move. Finally,* ELIZABETH *quietens, falls into* CREATURE*'s arms. Gone. All is silent for a beat until* CREATURE *sings the opening lines of 'You Are My Sunshine' by Jimmie Davis.* CREATURE *takes the mirror to* ELIZABETH*'s lips—no breath.*

CREATURE: So that's a 'no', then?

> VICTOR *walks to them, swaps places with* CREATURE, *holding* ELIZABETH *in his arms.*

VICTOR: Nothing is so painful to the human mind as a great and sudden change. The sun might shine, the clouds might lower, but nothing could appear to me as it had the day before. A fiend had snatched from me every hope of happiness; no-one had ever been so miserable as I; so frightful an event is single in the history of man.

CREATURE: Men, men, men.

> OTHERS *enter and remove* ELIZABETH *on a stretcher.* VICTOR *comes forward to us.*

VICTOR: My father sickened from grief.

> OTHERS *bring* FATHER *in wheelchair.*

The springs of existence suddenly gave way and in a few days he died.

> FATHER *dies.* CREATURE *moves to him, kisses him on the forehead.* OTHERS *wheel him out.*

I began to reflect on the cause of all this. The devil I had sent into the world for my own destruction.

CREATURE: [*to us*] That would be me.

VICTOR: I vowed revenge on her cursed head.

CREATURE: How ignorant you are in your pride. You know not what it is you say.

VICTOR: [*kneeling*] By the sacred earth on which I kneel, by the deep and eternal grief that I feel, I swear to pursue her, until she or I shall perish in mortal conflict. I call on you, spirits of the dead, and on you, wandering ministers of vengeance, to aid me in my work.

CREATURE: Men, so emotional. Am I right?

VICTOR: I was answered through the stillness of the night by a—

> CREATURE *laughs.*

It rang on my ears long and heavily; the mountains re-echoed it, I felt as if all hell surrounded me with mockery. A voice said ...

CREATURE: I am satisfied.

VICTOR: Suddenly the broad disc of the moon arose and shone full upon her ghastly and distorted shape as she fled with more than mortal speed.

> CREATURE *jumps on the scooter, rides around the space. During the following, the scene on the ship is re-established.* CAPTAIN ROBERT *enters, sits in a deckchair.*

I have pursued her for many months. Followed the windings of the River Rhone, the blue Mediterranean, the Black Sea. Amidst the wilds of Tartary and Russia she still evaded me.
CREATURE: Dasvidanya, comrade!

> OTHERS *hum a few lines of 'Song of the Volga Boat Men'—Russian folk song—as they return with the rope forming the ship as in the first scene.*

VICTOR: To you first entering on life, to whom care is new and agony unknown, how can you understand how I have felt and feel? Sometimes she left writing on the bark of trees.

> CREATURE *clicks remote—words projected—'my reign is not yet over'. She circles the ship on her scooter.* OTHERS *join her as her two* DOGS.

CREATURE: You live, and my power is complete.
OTHERS: Follow me.
CREATURE: I seek the everlasting ices of the north.
OTHERS: Come on.
CREATURE: Come on my enemy. We have yet to wrestle for our lives.
VICTOR: I cannot guess how many days have passed since then. I was almost within a grasp of my foe.

> VICTOR *reaches out a hand.*

CREATURE: Too weak—
VICTOR: Too weak. I was about to sink under the accumulation of distress when I saw your vessel riding at anchor. [*To* CAPTAIN ROBERT] Swear to me Captain that she shall not live.
CREATURE: How very dare you!
VICTOR: She is eloquent and persuasive but do not trust her. Her soul is full of treachery. Call on the names of—
WILLIAM: William—
JUSTINE: Justine—
HENRY: Henry—
ELIZABETH: Elizabeth—
FATHER: Father—
VICTOR: And thrust a sword into her heart.

> CREATURE *feigns being hurt.* CAPTAIN ROBERT *comes to us.*

ACT TWO 45

CAPTAIN ROBERT: His is the strangest tale that imagination ever formed. I wish to soothe him, yet I cannot.
VICTOR: I believed myself destined for some great enterprise. Man's power over man, life's triumph over death. I was foolish.
CREATURE: And utterly magnificent.
VICTOR: All my hopes are as nothing. Oh, how I am sunk.
CREATURE: [*loud and slow*] Myyyyyyyy turrrrrrrrrnnnnn.

> CREATURE *clicks remote—words projected—'let's finish this war'. She removes her other sock and shoe.*

SCENE TWELVE

CAPTAIN ROBERT *comes forward.*

CAPTAIN ROBERT: September ninth, the ice began to move, and roarings like thunder were heard at a distance as the islands split and cracked in every direction. My chief attention was occupied by my guest whose illness increased in such a degree that he was entirely confined to his bed.

> OTHER *brings in wheelchair.* OTHERS *transfer* VICTOR *to the wheelchair.*

He had not many hours to live. I sat by his bed, watching him.
CREATURE: The strength—
VICTOR: The strength I relied on is—
CREATURE: Going, going—
VICTOR: Gone. The forms of the beloved dead appear before me.
FATHER: We wait.
WILLIAM: We love you.
JUSTINE: Justice is served.
HENRY: Dear Frankenstein.
ELIZABETH: [*flat*] Yay.
VICTOR: I hasten to their arms. I regret everything and nothing.

> CREATURE *feigns playing a small violin.*

Farewell. Seek happiness in tranquillity and avoid ambition.
CAPTAIN ROBERT: He sank into silence.

> *All exit except* CREATURE *and* VICTOR. CREATURE *circles* VICTOR.

CREATURE: Oh Frankenstein, should I ask you now to pardon me?

> VICTOR *is so weak he cannot answer. He reaches out a hand.* CREATURE *takes it, kisses it.*

You are cold and cannot answer. Do you dream? Do you think I am dead to agony and remorse? Think you the groans of William, Justine, Henry and Elizabeth were music to my ears?

> VICTOR *cries out.*

I cast off all feeling. Subdued all anguish. Evil became my good. Now it is ending.

VICTOR: [*weakly*] Wretch.

> CREATURE *moves to him.*

CREATURE: A friend. I wanted a friend. I begged for a friend. Here, I said, hands out, this is where I shall hold my friend. Make her for me. Please. So little, so little to ask. And you … you threw a torch into a pile of buildings, and when they were consumed, you sat among the ruins and lamented the fall. You made me. Made me into the thing you hated most, the fallen angel, the enemy of God and man, *made* by God and man. I desired love, and I was spurned. Where was the justice in this? [*To us*] Am I the only sinner when all of you have sinned against me. [*To* VICTOR] You. You have sinned against me most. If I am a wretch, it is because you made me a wretch.

> CREATURE *moves behind* VICTOR, *arms across* VICTOR*'s chest.*

You fashioned me this way. Took pleasure in it. Celebrated your achievement. Me. Me. I have murdered the lovely and helpless. Strangled the innocent as they slept and grasped the throats of those who never injured me. I have damned you to misery, my creator, the select specimen of all that is worthy of admiration, I have damned you, damned you, damned you to misery. [*Caressing his hair*] You hate me, but that cannot equal how I regard myself. I look on the fingers which formed me; I think on the heart in which the imagination of it was conceived and long for the moment when these fingers will meet my eyes.

> CREATURE *moves away from* VICTOR, *to us.*

ACT TWO 47

I shall no longer see the sun or stars or feel the wind play on my cheeks. Light, feeling, and sense will pass; and in this condition I find the thing. Happiness. Years ago, when I felt rustling of leaves, singing of birds, I would have wept to die. Now I long for it. [*To* VICTOR] You. You made me into the thing the world hated most of all. [*Smiling*] A woman without fear.

>*Pause.*

A friend. All I wanted was a friend. So little, so little to ask.

>VICTOR *dies.* CREATURE *shakes him.*

Rise. Resist. Get up. Like Medusa with the bleeding head of Perseus, I don't want equality. I. Want. Revenge. [*Yelling*] Victor Frankenstein you shall not win!

>CREATURE *shakes him again. It's useless. It is over. She kisses him on the lips and moves from him. She slowly removes her trousers. Drops them to the floor. She now stands as she did when we first met her—in corset and bloomers. She calls her* DOGS. *They bring the scooter.*

Here it is. A ghost story just for you. Boo! A story of beasties that go bump and grind in the day and munch, munch, munch all through the endless night. Of those in human shape and those who are not, of those in shadow and those in light, of the tragedies of women and children and men, men, men.

>CREATURE *holds up her arms.* CAPTAIN ROBERT *and* OTHERS *enter with jumper leads. They attach the leads to* VICTOR's *arms and legs.*

CAPTAIN ROBERT: The death of Victor seemed so pointless. There must be another way to stem of the tide of mortality. My mind filled with one concept.

CREATURE: —

CAPTAIN ROBERT: One purpose.

>CREATURE *laughs.* CAPTAIN ROBERT *presses start button.* VICTOR *jerks but does not come to life.*

OTHER ONE: As my mother before me bore me.

OTHER TWO: As a pretty soldier of the earth.

CAPTAIN ROBERT: Clear!

> *Pushes button.* VICTOR *jerks but does not come to life.*

OTHER THREE: I will let her know all she is worth.
OTHER FOUR: For she must know above all things.
CAPTAIN ROBERT: Clear!

> CAPTAIN ROBERT *presses starter button.* VICTOR *jerks and comes to life. He rises, screams and freezes.*

CREATURE: I will sleep in peace. I will be borne away by the waves and lost in the darkness and distance.
None may endure.
Except.
For.
Me.

> OTHERS *bring* CREATURE *red lipstick. She smears it all over her face—warpaint.*

If you wish for happiness, for love, for something larger than a lie, you have been in the wrong place, my dear, dear ones, my hot-headed, heart-led babies.

> CREATURE *steps onto her scooter and rides. She clicks remote. Blackout. Words projected—'something resides in this heart that is not perishable—and life is more than a dream.'*

THE END

LA MAMA

presents

FRANKENSTEIN

Adapted by **Christine Davey**
Based on the novel by **Mary Shelley**

La Mama Courthouse
20–25 June, 2023

Cover photograph by: Darren Gill
Cover photo features: Tessa-Marie Luminati as The Creature

WRITER/DIRECTOR NOTES – CHRISTINE DAVEY

Frankenstein is a remarkable novel that beautifully lends itself to translation into resonating theatre for the 21st century. It is dark, stark and larger than life. Mary Shelley (1797–1851) was a supreme storyteller, and this production pays homage to her brilliance and bravery while advancing the thematic thread of the story—investigating love, loss, power, abuse of power and ultimately the complex nature of friendship. I feel the influence of Mary Wollstonecraft (Shelley's mother), the first modern feminist, in the formation of this production, as an influence on Mary, on me and on all women who come after her. At its heart this iteration of this story is unashamedly feminist—a screaming, clawing, fighting thing—a testament to resilience and the ongoing struggle for gender equity. Writing the adaptation of this heightened, dramatic and sweeping tale has been a joy. Helping the actors to make this tale their own has been a pleasure.

PRODUCTION NOTES

Background
This adaptation of *Frankenstein* began as an idea about power and how to translate the concept of power (and its abuses) into a contemporary, theatrical setting. Over a series of creative development workshops, the writer/director played with regionally based actors, dancers and theatre creatives as we ventured towards something tangible. The end result is a larger-than-life, singing, dancing, grotesquery of a script that pays respect to the tropes of Epic Theatre and breaks down the fourth wall between actor and audience.

Approach to the performance style, language and text

The play text is rich and textured, and the performance will be enhanced by sound, lighting, projections and movement, creating a feeling of pulsating forward movement to the whole. The narrative weaves in and out of the text, the sound, the movement and the images.

The text draws on the original source material of Shelley's novel, written in 1818, as well as infusing a contemporary commentary, involving the socio-politics of today.

This is a show about who we are and who we would like to be; about memory, truth and those we rely upon to speak. The Creature speaks directly to us, her companions and accomplices. She invites us on the journey, good and bad, happy and hideous. She is our leader and destroyer.

The production draws on tropes of horror, burlesque and science fiction. The approach borrows from Brechtian, Shakespearean and Greek Tragedies. It is funny, loud, tragic and transgressive.

Themes

Frankenstein is a cautionary tale about taking life for granted and the absolute corruption of absolute power. Victor Frankenstein creatures a 'creature/monster' because he wants to cheat death. The fall-out, however, is catastrophic. He creates without pause. He cheats death without thinking of the ramifications. Known as the first science fiction novel, Mary Shelley wrote *Frankenstein* as a dare—a ghost story. Her tale became that of a creature/monster let loose upon the world. The creature/monster could very well be her, be all of us—the uncontrollable 'thing' within.

This production approaches the story from a stridently feminist position—exploring the concept of the sidelined, the misunderstood, the trodden-on, the 'othered'. Thus, we have given our 'Creature/Monster' a gender. She is female. She is the thing the world hates the most—a woman without fear. She won't be put in a box or bent to conformity. That is what makes her dangerous.

Design: Set, Lighting, Sound, Music, Costumes, Use of IT and/or Projection

The design of *Frankenstein* is simple in order to allow space for a heightened performance style. Projections form a backdrop to the text, an addition to the storyline. Sound and music weave in and out of the story, sometimes disjointed, sometimes harmonious. Movement and dance join the text, taking the story further in a physical sense.

The world of the play is timeless and ageless. We pay little attention to gender (apart from the Creature/Monster) or age, ethnicity or ability. The entire world is created by nine actors inhabiting a myriad of roles and characters.

Ultimately the design of the play aims to establish a dream. We are in the dream, surrounded by the dream and we will leave the dream at the end of the play and head back into reality.

The set design is also transportable for touring.

WRITER'S ACKNOWLEDGEMENTS

Thanks to Liz Jones at La Mama for programming Frankenstein at La Mama Courthouse, as part of the La Mama Learning Program, as well as Maureen Hartley, La Mama Learning Producer. Thanks also to Caitlin Dullard and all at La Mama who have assisted this production. Thanks to Claire Grady, Katie Pollock and the team at Currency Press for all their assistance with the publication of this book, and to Adam Cass. Thanks to the original creatives who began the *Frankenstein* journey—Lauren Atkin, Steph Beall, Rachel Edmonds, Katie Hall, Glen Barton, Greg Chadwick, Taylah Broad, Elva Dandelion, Graci Lynch, Karen Long and Sarah Smits.

This adaptation of *Frankenstein* was first produced by La Mama at the La Mama Courthouse Theatre, Melbourne, on 20 June 2023, with the following cast:

VICTOR FRANKENSTEIN	Graci Lynch
THE CREATURE	Tessa-Marie Luminati
ELIZABETH/ENSEMBLE	Taylah Broad
FATHER/ENSEMBLE	Paula Kontelj
MOTHER/ENSEMBLE	Kerry Davies
WILLIAM/ENSEMBLE	Aly Jane
HENRY/ENSEMBLE	Danae Reid
OTHER CREATURE/ENSEMBLE	Lucia Kelly
CAPTAIN ROBERT/ENSEMBLE	Lauren Atkin

Writer/Director, Christine Davey
Assistant Director, Elva Dandelion
Costumes, Emma Jones
Design, Christine Davey

CEO & Artistic Director – Caitlin Dullard
Marketing and Communications – Georgina Capper
Development & Pathways Manager – Myf Powell
Venue Technical Manager – Hayley Fox
Producer & Front-of-House Manager – Amber Hart
First Nations Producer/ Curator – Glenn Shea
Learning Producer & School Publications Coordinator - Maureen Hartley
Ticketing & FOH Supervisors – Aya Taur & Gemma Horbury
Design & Marketing Admin – Adam Cass
On-line Producer – Ruiqi Fu

Curators:
Gemma Horbury (**Musica**); Amanda Anastasi (**Poetica**)
Isabel Knight (**Cabaretica**); Sophia Constantine (**La Mama for Kids**)
La Mama Elder – Liz Jones
Documentation – Darren Gill

La Mama Theatre & Office is at 205 Faraday St, Carlton VIC 3053
La Mama Courthouse Theatre, 349 Drummond Street, Carlton VIC 3053

www.lamama.com.au   email: info@lamama.com.au
Facebook: lamama.theatre   twitter: LaMamaTheatre
instagram: lamamatheatre

Office phone (03) 9347 6948
Office hours Mon–Fri, 11am–4pm.

FRONT OF HOUSE STAFF: Amber Hart, Maureen Hartley, Myf Powell, Laurence Strangio, Hayley Fox, Susan Bamford-Caleo, Dennis Coard, Isabel Knight, Dora Abraham, Ruiqi Fu, Sarah Corridon, Nicki Jam, Aya Taur, Andreas Petropoulos, Dani Hayek, Gemma Horbury, Helen Hopkins, Loukia Vassiliades, Lisa Inman, Maddie Nunn, and Jaye Syson.

COMMITTEE OF MANAGEMENT: Richard Watts (Chair), Helen Hopkins (Dep Chair), Ben Grant, (Treasurer) Caitlin Dullard (Secretary), Members: Caroline Lee, David Geoffrey Hall, Kim Ho, Beng Oh, Mark Williams and Liz Jones.

La Mama Theatre is on traditional land of the people of the Kulin Nation. We give our respect to the Elders of these traditional lands, and to all First Nations people, past and present, and future. We acknowledge all events take place on stolen lands and that sovereignty was never ceded.

La Mama is financially assisted by Creative Victoria (Creative Enterprises Program), and the City of Melbourne (Arts and Creative Partnership Program). We are grateful to all our philanthropic partners and donors, advocates, volunteers, audiences, artists and our entire community. Thank you!

CHRISTINE DAVEY
WRITER/DIRECTOR

Christine is a writer/director/producer of some 30 years' standing. Her previous adaptations of *My Brilliant Career* and *Jane Eyre* have been on the VCE syllabus as well as enjoying seasons at La Mama and various venues across regional Victoria. She has had four plays published, won awards such as the Wal Cherry, Bundanon Residency and Wheeler Centre Fellowship. Christine is artistic director of Skin of our Teeth Productions, has a PhD in creative writing and lectures at the University of Melbourne and Deakin University.

ELVA DANDELION
ASSISTANT DIRECTOR

Elva is an actor and director, graduating from Nepean University. She was most recently seen in SooT's production of *My Brilliant Career* at La Mama Courthouse in 2021. Elva has been immersed in an array of physical modalities and collaborative adaptions.

EMMA JONES
COSTUMES

Emma is an interior designer by day and has been involved in theatre for over 30 years. Emma has directed several plays and won awards for her costume design, including for SooT's 2015 production of *Pride and Prejudice*.

GRACI LYNCH
VICTOR FRANKENSTEIN

Graci has been involved with SOOT since 2014. She has enjoyed being a part of both production and stage teams and has worn many hats (stage manager/director/associate director/actor). Notable acting credits include *Macbeth* (Witch), *A Midsummer Night's Dream* (Titania) and *Loves Labour's Won* (Dogberry) where she won a VDL for best actress in a minor role. This year is a bumper one for her. She is involved in three SooT shows across the season. She is very excited to be a part of the mad and crazy world of *Frankenstein*.

TESSA-MARIE LUMINATI
THE CREATURE

Tessa is an actor/theatre-maker who completed a Bachelor of Acting for Stage and Screen at Federation University in 2018. Tessa has been exploring Suzuki and theatre-making techniques in the Melbourne-based ensemble The Thursday Group. She worked and trained with physical theatre company 5 Angry Men. She performed in *Multitud*, directed by Tamara Cubas as part of Melbourne's Rising Festival and has just come back from MAP Fest in Malaysia to perform her solo show *The Waves*.

TAYLAH BROAD
ELIZABETH/ENSEMBLE

Taylah has enjoyed performing from a young age and shares this passion with her students in the classroom as a drama teacher at Christian College Geelong. In 2022, she enjoyed assistant directing and stage managing *Shrek The Musical*. She graduated from Deakin University in 2019 and is excited to be involved in such a compelling and thought-provoking adaption of *Frankenstein* that critiques/rejects traditional standards of beauty and the objectification of woman.

PAULA KONTELJ
FATHER/ENSEMBLE

Paula has worked in commercial radio for more than 25 years and in theatre both here and the Channel Islands. This is her second production with SooT, having previously performed in *My Brilliant Career* (La Mama, 2021). Paula is excited to switch genders in *Frankenstein*. The last time she did that was in 1979 playing one of the brothers in *Joseph and the Amazing Technicolour Dreamcoat* in her Geelong High School production!

KERRY DAVIES
MOTHER/ENSEMBLE

Kerry has been creating theatre for more than 25 years and has a Diploma of Arts in Small Companies & Community Theatre and Bachelor of Arts majoring in Drama. She founded award winning theatre company Cheshire CAT in Geelong before working in Melbourne and Sydney.

ALY JANE
WILLIAM/ENSEMBLE

DANAE REID
HENRY/ENSEMBLE

Alysha recently graduated from the Australian Institute of Music with a Bachelor of Music in Musical Theatre in 2022. Their credits include self-produced cabarets *Teenage Dream* and *Wish You Were Gay* (with Riley Davey), William Barfee in *The 25th Annual Putnam County Spelling Bee* (AIM), and a featured role in YouTube comedy duo Superwog's *On A Plane* episodes. Aly first worked with SooT on *Worlds Where Life Might Exist*, and is thrilled to make their professional debut in *Frankenstein*.

Danae is a passionate, queer maker and shaker who lives/plays on Wadawarrung land (Geelong). She debuted in 2022 with *Attempts on Her Life* by Split Focus Productions. She graduated from The VCA in 2016 with a Bachelor of Fine Arts (Production). Since then, she has toured Australia with shows including *Matilda*, *Aladdin*, *Billy Elliot*, *Harry Potter and the Cursed Child* and *The Picture of Dorian Gray*.

LUCIA KELLY
OTHER CREATURE/ ENSEMBLE

Lucia studied at AC and Deakin University in a double degree in Secondary Education/ Performing Arts. At Deakin she was a part of Burwood Student Theatre Company. She also played Ursula in *Much Ado About Nothing* (2017), *Diane in Blackrock* (2017), and Mistress Slowly in *This Rose Has Thorns* (2018) She recently played Hamlet in *Hamlet* with the Grover Theatre Company (2022).

LAUREN ATKIN
CAPTAIN ROBERT/ ENSEMBLE

Lauren has been a part of the Geelong theatre scene since 2017. She has been in various productions with SooT and local theatre companies. With SooT she played a Witch in *Macbeth* (2017), Lucy Honeychurch in *A Room with a View* (2018) and Helen in *Jane Eyre* (2019). Lauren is looking forward to working with this creative brunch of theatre makers and shakers.

STANDING OVATION FOR AUSTRALIA'S HOME OF INDEPENDENT THEATRE

In 2023, La Mama celebrates 56 years of nurturing new Australian Theatre, fearlessly facilitating independent theatre making.

Built in 1883 for Anthony Reuben Ford, a Carlton printer, the original building in Faraday Street had been used as a workshop, a boot and shoe factory, an electrical engineering workshop and a silk underwear factory before becoming a theatre in 1967. It was established by Betty Burstall and modelled on experimental theatre activities in New York. Jack Hibberd's play *Three Old Friends* was the first play performed in the tiny space. Since that time the crowded intimacy of La Mama has provided welcome opportunities to a host of playwrights, actors, directors, technicians, film-makers, poets and comedians, such as David Williamson, Barry Dickins, John Romeril, Tes Lyssiotis, Lloyd Jones, the Cantrills, Judith Lucy, Richard Frankland, Julia Zemiro, and Cate Blanchett... the list of both new and experienced theatre makers, and those artists who have been nurtured there, is long.

I set La Mama up, as a space for writers and directors to perform in but also it was a space where people came, as audience, to participate in the creative experiment...

—Betty Burstall, 1987

La Mama Theatre—which on various occasions has been called headquarters, the shopfront and the birthplace of Australian Theatre—was classified by the National Trust in 1999.

The two-storey brick building is of State cultural significance because it has been occupied by La Mama Theatre...The building is indelibly associated with the performance arts and is a rare manifestation of an experimental theatre in Australia...
—National Trust Classification Report

Sadly our home in Faraday Street burned down in May 2018 and, while we were in the process of rebuilding, our home was La Mama Courthouse on Drummond Street Carlton.

Happily, like a phoenix rising from the ashes, our rebuilt La Mama Theatre was reopened in December, 2021 with the War-Rak/ Banksia Festival. (For rebuild details see https://lamama.com.au/rebuild-la-mama)

During its 50-plus years, La Mama has presented approximately 2,500 shows, and we now average around 50 primary production seasons annually, as well as developments, seasonal La Mamica events (Musica, Poetica, Cabaretica, Kids' shows), regular touring through our Mobile program, plus our VCE Learning productions, play readings, and many other special events.

Performances take place again in the restored La Mama, and continue at our second performance venue, the refurbished La Mama Courthouse, 349 Drummond Street.

An ever-increasing audience is drawn to La Mama productions, not only from the Carlton and Melbourne University environs, but from far and wide across the country.

La Mama continues to be an open, accessible space, actively breaking down barriers to the Arts through diverse programs, creative initiatives, affordable ticketing, improved accessible amenities and a welcoming ethos, for performers and audience alike, that has developed over the past five decades. La Mama is home to many and open to all.

For details of all productions and events, and bookings visit: www.lamama.com.au

www.currency.com.au

Visit Currency Press' website now to:
- Buy your books online
- Browse through our full list of titles, from plays to screenplays, books on theatre, film and music, and more
- Choose a play for your school or amateur performance group by cast size and gender
- Obtain information about performance rights
- Find out about theatre productions and other performing arts news across Australia
- For students, read our study guides
- For teachers, access syllabus and other relevant information
- Sign up for our email newsletter

The performing arts publisher

www.ingramcontent.com/pod-product-compliance
Lightning Source LLC
Chambersburg PA
CBHW050024090426
42734CB00021B/3405